ENGLAND
WALES - SCOTLAND

Text by David Mountfield

Crescent Books

A division of Crown Publishers, Inc.

Above, view of the harbour at Brixham, Devon.
Right, the Horse Guards on parade in London.

First English edition published by Editions Minerva S.A., Genève

Library of Congress Catalog
Card Number: DA684.2M68 942.1'2 79-9796

I.S.B.N. 0-517-28277-1

This edition is distributed by Crescent Books,
a division of Crown Publishers, Inc.

a   b   c   d   e   f   g   h

© *Editions Minerva., Genève, 1979*
Printed in Italy.

LONDON

London is one of the most attractive of all great capital cities, both for visitors and for residents. Although it is so large, disproportionately so, many non-Londoners feel, it is not overpowering, as it consists of a collection of linked "villages" grouped around the metropolitan focus points provided by the West End (containing the main hotels, restaurants, museums and shops) and the City, the business and financial district. The various sections, or "villages", have a distinctive character of their own, and remain surprisingly self-contained, though this pleasant characteristic depends on the less desirable fact of London's vast extent: the area controlled by the Greater London Council comprises 1580 square kilo-metres, and the "urban sprawl", though relieved by a "green belt" (area of no construction), extends much farther than that. In recent years London has lost some of its varied and intimate character with the appearance of large modern buildings of the type that have disfigured many another old European city. In size, shape and materials, the modern office and apartment blocks inevitably clash with the traditional environment, and not all architects have succeeded in reducing this jarring note to an acceptable minimum. There have also been some scandals, like that of Centre Point, a huge office tower on a central site which, for reasons best understood by its owners' lawyers and accountants, remain-

The Houses of Parliament, Victoria Tower and Big Ben.

ed empty and unlet many years after its completion.

The traditional "square mile" of the City is the oldest inhabited area, roughly corresponding with the walled town of the Middle Ages. Its eastern boundary is marked by the Tower of London, built by the Normans in the late 11th century. In 1666 most of the area within the wall was destroyed in the Great Fire, and medieval remains in London are therefore comparatively few. One church that survived is St Bartholomew's, Smithfield, originally part of an Augustinian priory, while Westminster, along with other areas already built-up beyond the medieval walls, were untouched by the Fire. One advantage of the catastrophe was that it presented an outstanding architect, Christopher Wren, with unrivalled opportunities, and although questions of land-ownership prevented his great plans for redesigning the city on more spacious lines being carried out, his influence remains paramount in London's architecture.

The second greatest disaster for London's historical fabric was the "Blitz" of the Second World War, when Hitler attempted to bomb the capital into submission. The few medieval guild halls which had survived the Fire of 1666 were largely destroyed, though many have since been lovingly restored. Damage elsewhere, especially in the poor districts of the East End and the Docks, was very extensive, though looking at London today it is surprising to see how little evidence of the destruction of 1940-45 remains. Even the Blitz had its compensations, for the devastated areas yielded some remarkable archaeological finds, including a Roman temple to Mithras, now restored using the original materials.

London's dual function as the seat of government and centre of commerce grew up with a healthy distance dividing them, the former in Westminster and the latter in the City, with the River Thames providing the highway between them. Of the old palace of Westminster the main survival is the 14th-century Westminster Hall, with its remarkable hammerbeam timber roof. The Houses of Parliament replaced the old Palace in the mid- 19th century; they are a strikingly successful result of a somewhat uneasy collaboration—the Gothicism of Augustus Pugin and the Classicism of Sir Charles Barry. Most of the stonework has been renewed in recent years following damage by air pollution; nowadays, thanks to the Clean Air Act, the old London "pea-soup" fog is but a memory. Inside, the House of Lords is particularly opulent; the Commons' chamber was rebuilt after destruction by fire in 1941. The clock tower, familiarly known as Big Ben (though the name strictly belongs to the bell, named after the contemporary Commissioner of Works) is London's most popular symbol, closely followed by another spectacular piece of Victorian Gothic, Tower Bridge.

Westminster Abbey, scene of nationally important religious ceremonies such as the coronation of a sovereign, was founded, according to legend, by St Peter himself. The English once believed that they were God's Chosen People, the Jews having proved a disappointment, and legends that ascribed the founding of Christianity in England to one of the Apostles—some said Christ himself—were encouraged after the Protestant Reformation of the 16th century, when it was politic to denigrate any obligation to Rome. There was an abbey here before the Norman Conquest, but almost nothing of it is left. The present building

Right, a theatre in the Strand. London has a more active theatrical life than any other capital city. Bottom, a famous pub frequented mainly by lawyers. Far right, Piccadilly Circus by night.

dates from the mid-13th century onwards, and includes the famous 16th-century chapel of Henry VII, apotheosis of the English late Gothic style, with scintillating fan vaulting. The Abbey is like a picture book of English history, containing many tombs and memorials of the famous; a special place, "Poets' Corner", is reserved for literary figures.

Not very far from the Abbey is the corresponding headquarters of Roman Catholicism, Westminster Cathedral, built at the end of the 19th century, rather incongruously, in Byzantine style. Its bell tower, which once offered unrivalled views, is now partly blocked by the office buildings of Victoria.

As Parliament Square is the centre of Westminster, the heart of the City is to be found in the crowded space where six streets come together in the shadow of the Bank of England and, across the way, the Bank underground railway station daily disgorges its hordes of "City gents" in sober suits, a few still wearing the familiar bowler hat. The buildings here—the Bank itself, the Royal Exchange (now superseded by the newer Stock Exchange nearby), and the Mansion House (official residence of the Lord Mayor)—are Neo-Classical in design and imposing in appearance, though perhaps the more attractive aspects of the City are its little courts and alleys where, on deserted Sundays, many quaint architectural details reward the persevering explorer.

The district of London which offers most to the visitor—many of whom hardly realise that anything exists outside it—is the West End, of which Piccadilly Circus forms the hub. To the north of the Circus, with its statue of Eros and its circling "double-decker" buses, lie Shaftesbury Avenue, lined with theatres, Regent Street, a moderately grand shopping street, and between them Soho, a cramped, colourful, seedy district of good restaurants and doubtful nightclubs, bounded on the north by Oxford Street, where the great department stores stand shoulder to shoulder. To the west is fashionable Mayfair, with its expensive hotels, grand embassies, Georgian houses, and some reminders of a less exclusive past in places like Shepherd Market, a little "village" of narrow streets and small shops. South-east is Trafalgar Square, a spacious area which was claimed by John Nash from narrow streets and slums in a 19th-century redevelopment, dominated by the tall column supporting a statue of England's premier naval hero, Lord Nelson. South-west is St James's, containing the royal palace once the chief residence of the monarch (ambassadors are still appointed "to the Court of St James's") and many exclusive private clubs.

Although London extends far beyond them, most of the attractions of a great capital city are to be found within these three areas—Westminster, the City and the West End. In spite of the innumerable great institutions and magnificent individual buildings, much of London's charm derives from its domestic architecture, which is mainly 18th and 19th century. Typical Georgian (18th-century) brick housing, three or four storeys high and totally unpretentious except for the doorways, still survives in considerable quantity, for example in Bedford Square. Considerably grander are the gracious white terraces of Nash (1752-1835), best seen on the east side of Regent's Park. Elsewhere, even among the elegant shops of Regent Street, little remains of the work of London's most able and ambitious planner after Wren. As for Wren himself, his eclectic genius

is best seen in the astonishing variety of City churches (of which he built about fifty), basically simple buildings but almost every one possessing a steeple of unique and charming form. The greatest of Wren's ecclesiastical buildings, of course, is St Paul's Cathedral, a massive church in a restrained version of Baroque, topped by a serene and magnificent dome. St Paul's is the chief church of London (Westminster Abbey belongs to the whole nation), and Wren's building replaced an enormous, rambling Gothic structure, destroyed in the Fire of 1666. Of his secular buildings, most notable are Chelsea Hospital, where old soldiers are cared for in their declining days, and a similarly intended, much grander hospital for sailors, now part of the Royal Naval College at Greenwich, adjacent to the National Maritime Museum.

The collection of the National Maritime Museum, including a famous old clipper ship, the *Cutty Sark,* is well worth a trip down the river in one of the boats from Westminster Bridge or the Tower. London is well provided with museums and art galleries. The National Gallery, whose facade forms the north side of Trafalgar Square, contains one of the finest collections of

Top left, one of the most popular tourist sights in London, opposite Nelson's Column. Bottom, the Tower of London. Above, Tower Bridge.

paintings in the world. Historians find the National Portrait Gallery, around the corner, no less interesting. For modern paintings, one must enter the ornate portals of the Tate Gallery, on the river near the Millbank Tower, one of the more attractive additions to the modern skyline. The Hayward Gallery, among the concrete complex of cultural buildings on the South Bank, houses temporary art exhibitions. The crowds at these galleries sometimes appear intimidating, but they tend to gather most densely at the prints and postcards counter in the foyer, permitting easy progress in the galleries.

The most impressive museum in London is the British Museum, a vast Neo-Classical edifice in Bloomsbury, a favourite district for writers, whose research can be undertaken in the 6,000,000 volumes of the British Library (soon to move into new premises). The British Museum also contains Egyptian mummies, sculpture from the Parthenon, treasures from Iron-Age Britain, and thousands of other marvellous artifacts. The Wallace Collection, in Manchester Square, surprisingly neglected, is particularly strong in French works.

There is a cluster of museums in South Kensington, including the Natural History Museum and—favourite of most Londoners—the Victoria and Albert, a huge collection of fine and —especially—applied arts, which includes such curiosities as the "Great Bed of Ware", capable of sleeping eight, and mentioned by Shakespeare. The new London Museum, with its brilliant survey of London's history, is in the Barbican project, a recent attempt to bring back permanent inhabitants to the City.

Of specialised museums, several have a military connection. The Imperial War Museum, south of the river in Southwark, is the finest; it was once

used as a lunatic asylum. At Hyde Park Corner the house of England's greatest soldier, the Duke of Wellington, is now a museum devoted to his career. Several literary and artistic figures are similarly commemorated in their former residences—Carlyle in Cheyne Row, Dickens in Doughty Street, Hogarth in Chiswick, Samuel Johnson off Fleet Street (still the centre of the newspaper industry), Keats in Hampstead. For some people, the most charming of all private residences is Horace Walpole's villa at Strawberry Hill, Twickenham, one of the first manifestations of the 18th-century Gothic Revival, now part of a teachers' training college.

Royal palaces are surprisingly numerous in and near London. Buckingham Palace, the modern official royal residence, was enlarged and remodelled by Nash; the art gallery and the mews, where the gold coronation coach is kept, attract many visitors. St James's Palace has a ceiling by Holbein, Kensington Palace is cosy and domestic, Kew Palace is simply a 17th-century Dutch cottage. More of the royal art collection is on view at Hampton Court Palace, a brick building in the style, plain and relaxed (except for contorted chimneys), of the 16th century, with additions by Wren, and at Windsor Castle, in Berkshire, the best-preserved Norman castle in England. Queen Victoria found the bedrooms "pokey" but at least her windows were not

rattled by Concorde, ascending from London Airport.

Though short of medieval buildings, London has many churches (besides the cathedrals mentioned above) of special interest. All Souls, Langham Place, is famous for Nash's spiky spire; Brompton Oratory, in Knightsbridge, is a remarkable example of the late 19th-century Italianate revival; St George's, Hanover Square, is the scene of high-society weddings; St Martin-in-the-Fields (1726) is the masterpiece of James Gibbs and an influential example of classical portico combined with "Gothic" spire; St Mary-le-Bow is some people's favourite Wren church, though others prefer St Stephen, Walbrook; Southwark Cathedral is basically a large medieval church, much rebuilt.

Other famous London landmarks include the Banqueting House, Whitehall (1620), by Inigo Jones, with ceiling by Rubens; Burlington House, which contains various learned societies including the Royal Academy of Art; Chiswick House, a domed villa in the English Palladian style; the Inns of Court, home of the legal profession; Guildhall, a medieval building much restored; Holland House, unofficial headquarters of the Whig party in the 19th century; the Law Courts in the Strand, in attractive Victorian Gothic; Somerset House, the vast 18th-century office building with a 250-metres river frontage;

Left, a London square; London's parks have always been one of its major delights. Centre, two typical London street scenes.

Osterley Park and Syon House, two fine old houses to the south-west which provide some of the best examples of the work of the famous 18th-century Scottish architect-designer, Robert Adam.

The best view of London is from the revolving restaurant in the Post Office Tower, the highest building, and from there it is easy to appreciate the benefits London enjoys from its "lungs" —the parks and gardens. Hyde Park, Green Park and St James's were once part of royal hunting preserves, as was Regent's Park, laid out by Nash, which contains the London Zoo and a boating pool. Of wilder aspect are Hampstead Heath in the north, which includes the "stately home" of Kenwood, now national property, and Richmond Park in the south, with deer and magnificent views of the Thames valley. Wimbledon Common with its windmill, is the home of those mythical creatures loved by children, the "Wombles". The Royal Botanic Gardens at Kew, brilliant in the spring, contain large and splendid Victorian glasshouses and a tall Chinese pagoda. To the southwest, Bushey Park merges into the elegant gardens of Hampton Court, with a famous maze and a vine of incredible antiquity.

Londoners, even nowadays, are fond of traditional shows and pageants. The Changing of the Guard at Buckingham Palace is regularly observed by a knot of interested tourists, but it is necessary to apply for permission to see the nightly ceremony of the keys, when the gates are locked at the Tower, and for the Trooping of the Colour, on Horse Guards Parade on the Queen's birthday, most places are booked a year in advance. A big event in the City is the annual Lord Mayor's Show, when the new Lord Mayor travels in his gilded coach from Guildhall to the Royal

Courts, followed by ingenious "floats" and accompanied by liverymen and others in ancient uniforms. Many other arcane customs have lingered through the centuries, such as the ceremony of Maundy Thursday, when royal charity to the poor is symbolized by the Queen distributing specially minted silver coins at Westminster Abbey, or "swan-upping", when two City companies, the Dyers and the Vintners, go out in barges on the river to mark the beaks of the swans which by long tradition belong to them rather than, as other swans, to the sovereign. The Queen enjoys (or is perhaps thoroughly bored by) a number of quaint privileges that continue because no one can bring himself to stop them, such as the payment annually by the City of London of a billhook, a hatchet and six horseshoes —this being the rent due for some land in Shropshire.

One area in which the English have been remarkably fertile is the devising of popular sports and games (Pall Mall is named after the 17th-century game, a rough cross between golf and croquet, played there by the king), and this is reflected in the existence of internationally known sporting centres in London. The ultimate ambition of tennis players is to win the championship at Wimbledon; Twickenham is the "Mecca" of rugby football, and Lord's, in St John's Wood, of cricket. International soccer matches are played at Wembley, also the scene of athletics and show-jumping events, while the many London clubs have their own grounds scattered about. Indoor sports and other leisure activities are held at Olympia (Hammersmith), Earls Court or the Albert Hall, the circular concert hall where the light-hearted Promenade concerts are held each summer, which stands opposite London's largest

and most ornate monument to a single individual, the Albert Memorial. There is rowing on the Thames—the main event is the annual race between Oxford and Cambridge universities—and "real" tennis at Queen's Club and at Hampton Court; the court there dates from the time of King Henry VIII, a keen player.

Most of the main London theatres are within a few minutes' walk of Piccadilly Circus. The home of the Royal Shakespeare Company is in Aldwych, close to Bush House (home of the foreign service of the British Broadcasting Corporation), though the Company will soon move into a new theatre in the Barbican, and the National Theatre has three auditoriums in the new building on the South Bank, close to Waterloo. Other interesting or off-beat theatres are Covent Garden, home of opera and ballet; the Round House, a converted railway shed in Chalk Farm; the Royal Court, presenting avant-guarde productions in bohemian Chelsea; the Coliseum, largest theatre in London, mainly for opera and ballet; and the Mermaid, a converted riverside warehouse in Blackfriars.

Before the first theatres were built, plays were performed in inn courtyards. The George in Southwark is the last survivor of an inn of that type, with surrounding gallery. There is an inn or "pub" (public house) on every corner, it seems, and some of the most attractive are the least well known, found in backstreets off the beaten track. Restaurants are international, with Indian and Chinese predominant at the lower end of the price range particularly. Traditional English fare can be sampled in a place like Simpson's in the Strand, one of the few restaurants that serves roast saddle of mutton—every bit as good as the better-known roast beef.

The man who is tired of London, said that great Londoner Samuel Johnson, is tired of life. Truly, London contains amusement and stimulation for everyone, even though the best-known shops or restaurants may strain the purse of the average visitor, or the average Cockney (i.e. Londoner, but, strictly, an East Ender, born "within the sound of Bow bells"). Thanks partly to the international weakness of the English pound, London is not, nevertheless, a very expensive city, and woolens may be bought at Marks and Spencer as well as Harrods; a "pub" lunch is as nourishing as the more elegant cuisine at Mirabelle, Rules or Leith's; a "bed-and-breakfast" lodging house in Bayswater may be scarcely less comfortable or convenient than a suite at Claridges or the Savoy.

THE SOUTH-EAST

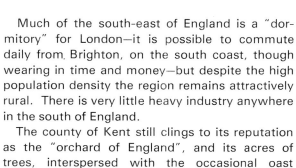

Much of the south-east of England is a "dormitory" for London—it is possible to commute daily from Brighton, on the south coast, though wearing in time and money—but despite the high population density the region remains attractively rural. There is very little heavy industry anywhere in the south of England.

The county of Kent still clings to its reputation as the "orchard of England", and its acres of trees, interspersed with the occasional oast house (a conical kiln for drying hops; some have been converted into charming if unconventional dwellings) make an attractive sight in apple-blossom time.

Kent was apparently settled largely by a Germanic people called the Jutes, and the traditional division between "men of Kent", from east of the Medway, and "Kentish men", from west of that river, may stem from the old division between Saxons and Jutes. The old kingdom of Kent was markedly different from other Anglo-Saxon kingdoms in its laws and customs, the absence of a law of primogeniture encouraging the growth of a sturdy yeoman class and militat-

Left, a quintessential English country town: Arundel, in Sussex. Below, white cliffs at Dover.

ing against the domination of great landowners. In other respects too Kent differs from its immediate neighbours; when an inch of snow falls in London, parts of Kent are likely to be snowed under.

The two main geographical features of Kent are the Weald, originally a forest and still well-timbered, which covers a large part of Kent and Sussex, and Romney March, behind the southern shore, a bleak area grazed by sheep and traversed by old smugglers' trails. The Weald once contained many iron works; that industry has been dead for over a century, but some coal is still mined in the east. Oil refineries have sprung up, and there is a vast nuclear power station at Dungeness.

Dover, with its Norman castle (still in military use) and Roman lighthouse tower, is the main gateway to the continent, though a more rapid passage can be made by hovercraft from the pleasant seaside resort of Ramsgate. The main road from Dover to London passes through Canterbury, which no doubt helps to account for Canterbury's popularity with visitors from abroad. The cathedral, seat of the archbishop of Canterbury, primate of the Church of England, was founded by St Augustine in 597 and rebuilt in Norman times. The murder of St Thomas Becket in 1170 made Canterbury a place of pilgrimage (Chaucer's pilgrims were bound there in the *Canterbury Tales*). One of the most magnificent English cathedrals, Canterbury is particularly notable for its stained glass.

The long coastline of Kent stretches from the Thames estuary around the North Foreland to Dungeness. Whitstable is famous for its oysters. Margate is a jolly, even raucous, seaside resort popular with Londoners. Broadstairs is more

Canterbury Cathedral.

refined, once favoured by Dickens and now a popular yachting centre. At Richborough the invading Romans built a port. Sandwich is one of the Cinque Ports (the others are Dover, Romney, Hythe and Hastings, but only Dover is still a port) which had a special role in defence during the Middle Ages. Deal has a fine beach and one of the most interesting of the series of coastal forts built in the reign of Henry VIII (1508-47) on the plan of interlocking circles —quite unlike earlier castles. Folkestone is a favourite watering place for the elderly and well-to-do, with a fine promenade from which the French coast is sometimes visible.

The county town of Kent is not Canterbury but Maidstone, which contains a palace once belonging to the archbishop of Canterbury and an interesting museum of coaches. Tunbridge Wells was a fashionable spa in the 18th century; today its name enshrines prosperous, middle-class respectability. Near the pleasant dormitory town of Sevenoaks is the magnificent palace of Knole, one of the largest private houses in England, begun in the 15th century. Other places of unusual interest are Leeds Castle, a "fairy castle" on an island in a lake; Sissinghurst Gardens, created by the writer V. Sackville-West; Igtham Mote, a medieval, moated manor house; and Charles Darwin's house at Downe, where he wrote the *Origin of Species.*

Surrey, flanking London on the south, is one of the smallest counties, though its population is large and growing. It is crossed, east to west, by the chalk ridge of the North Downs. Substantial woodland survives as well as many farms, and there are few large towns of character. Guildford, where Lewis Carroll is buried, is an old market town with an attractive main street and a university. Kingston-upon-Thames is older—football is said to have been invented there by Saxons kicking around the head of a dead Viking —but its character has changed since it became a centre of the commuter belt.

The smaller towns and villages, like Shere, Betchworth or Lingfield, reveal English domestic architecture at its most picturesque. Village inns are especially rewarding in Surrey. There are magnificent gardens at Wisley and at Polesdon Lacey, where there is also an open-air theatre. At Burford Bridge, at the foot of Box Hill, Nelson spent his last night ashore before the Battle of Trafalgar (1805). Runnymede, near Egham, is the place where, in 1215, King John was compelled to sign Magna Carta—the foundation of English civil liberties as it was subsequently interpreted. At Compton, near Guildford, there is a gallery devoted to the work of the Victorian painter G.F. Watts, and nearby his little, Art-Nouveau mausoleum. At Epsom, England's greatest horse race, the Derby, has been run annually since 1780. Hindhead, which William Cobbett in his *Rural Rides* (1830) called "the most villainous spot God ever made" hardly deserves such condemnation; from Gibbet Hill, nearly three hundred metres up, there is a fine view of Surrey heaths and woods. Ham House, near Richmond, contains a good collection of 17th-century furniture.

The Surrey countryside, so accessible from London, amply repays a day's touring. Distances are short, the pubs are welcoming (when open), and the sights are varied. But such a trip is best undertaken outside the holiday season, when traffic jams may be avoided.

Sussex, the much larger county to the south, is rather similar in character, but wilder. Only

two centuries ago parts of Sussex were surprisingly remote, isolated by notoriously bad roads, and some villages were terrorized by large gangs of smugglers. A trace of this turbulent past may be detected in the varied atmosphere of Sussex villages: though most are well-kept, prosperous, and thoroughly "southern" in the derogatory sense that a northerner uses the word, implying effeteness, a few appear rather scruffy and down-at-heel. There are few sizeable towns except on or near the coast; Crawley New Town is one exception and Horsham, old and picturesque, is another.

Topographically, the main feature in Sussex is the South Downs, rolling chalk uplands where the wind blows sharp, that reach across the county from Hampshire, gradually drawing closer to the sea until they break off in the famous "white cliffs" at Beachy Head. The Downs attract botanists and bird-watchers, as well as country-walkers.

The best-known town in Sussex is Brighton, once a small fishing village, now a major seaside resort in the summer and, in the winter, a conference centre. Brighton was made fashionable at the end of the 18th century by the Prince Regent (later George IV), a gentleman of ostentatious elegance, who commissioned the building of the Royal Pavilion. As redesigned by John Nash about 1812, this is one of the most remarkable buildings in England—an oriental palace owing most to the Mughal style of India, a mass of domes, minarets and fretted screens, with Chinese interiors. Much scorned at the time, it is still a bit of a joke, though few would deny its elegant charm. Round about are fine Georgian houses, narrow streets with antique shops, large and majestic hotels, two piers and other seaside

Top, one of the largest hotels in Brighton and Nash's Royal Pavilion.   Bottom, low water at Rye, and the venerable 12th-century church of Herstmonceaux, Sussex.

attractions. Neighbouring coastal towns, such as Worthing, Eastbourne and Hastings, are rather more sedate, favourite places for retirement (Worthing's citizens have the highest average age of any town in England). An old port of great charm is Rye, where the house of Henry James is sometimes open to the public; its steep cobbled streets are lined with interesting old houses. At Arundel there is what appears to be a well-

Left, Bodiam Castle, Sussex. Above, the village of Hastings; the fateful battle was actually fought some ten miles to the northwest. Below, landscape near Eastbourne.

preserved Norman castle, but much of it is 19th-century work; it is still inhabited by the Duke of Norfolk, whose forbears also built the impressive Roman Catholic church in French Gothic style. Chichester was an important place in Roman times: a 16th-century cross marks the junction of two Roman roads. Chichester cathedral, on the site of a Saxon church, has been much restored.

Many Sussex villages, with their greens and cricket pitches, weather-tiled gables, pitched roofs and old churches (some of Saxon origin) have great individual charm. Steyning is a not untypical example of a compact market town where little seems to have changed since the

18th century, though roads adequate for stage-coaches hardly cope with modern lorries. Among other attractive places are Petworth, a pretty town at the gates of a splendid 17th-18th century house with pictures by Van Dyck and others; the handicraft museum in a 15th-century timber-framed house at Bramber, which also has a ruined castle guarding a gap in the Downs; Battle Abbey, built by William the Conqueror to mark his victory in 1066; moated Bodiam Castle, which rivals Leeds Castle as the most romantic building in the south-east; the yachting centre of Bosham; Glyndebourne, home of a famous opera house; Herstmonceux Castle, a 15th-century brick build-ing which houses the Royal Observatory; the

Top, the Round Table of King Arthur and his twenty-four knights, at Winchester. Bottom, memorial to the Pilgrim Fathers at Southampton.

magnificent 19th-century Gothic chapel of Lancing College, near Worthing; and Winchelsea, with medieval gateways and fine Georgian houses.

The only substantial surviving part of the forests which once covered most of southern England is the New Forest in Hampshire. Quiet glades with wild ponies and ancient groves of oak and beech reward the summer campers. But much of Hampshire is high chalk uplands, while in the green meadows beside such rivers as Itchen, Test and Avon, anglers stalk trout, chub and roach, and in the sandy heaths of the north-east, a few Scots pines stand in gloomy silence. The Isle of Wight, reached by a short trip in ferry or hovercraft, is a summer resort retaining much Victorian charm.

The varied countryside, especially the forest, makes Hampshire an interesting county for naturalists; wild deer and ponies are an occasional traffic hazard on some roads. The famous 18th-century naturalist, Gilbert White, lived in Selborne; his house and garden are preserved as a museum. Jane Austen was another Hampshire resident; she wrote *Pride and Prejudice* at Steventon, though the house has gone.

The old city of Winchester was the capital of England in Saxon times; a statue of King Alfred stands guard over the town. Winchester cathedral, standing among green lawns, is one of the most impressive buildings in England, generating a powerful atmosphere, though architecturally a less-than-perfect specimen. Important Saxon and Roman remains have been discovered on this ancient site. The splendid nave is due to William of Wykeham, founder also of a boys' school, Winchester College (1382, earlier than Eton).

Street in Portsmouth. Below, the beach at Boscombe, Bournemouth.

The Hampshire coast is packed with shipping. Southampton is the major port for ocean liners in southern England, while Portsmouth is a large naval base. Southampton is big enough to have acquired many of the social problems that afflict modern industrial cities, though much evidence of its long maritime history is still evident. Portsmouth's vast dockyards find room for the proud old flagship of Admiral Nelson, the *Victory*. Bournemouth, in the west, makes a striking contrast with its busy neighbours, being essentially an elegant resort, with a fine symphony orchestra, extensive gardens and piers, but few pubs. Christchurch, a small, bustling town, has a magnificent Priory church. Beaulieu Abbey is today more famous for Lord Montague's museum of motor cars than for its Cistercian abbey, in part of which the motor-loving peer resides. The village of Hambledon, 20 km north of Portsmouth, was largely responsible for the develop-

Cowes, Isle of Wight, the chief yachting centre in the country.

ment of the modern game of cricket in the 18th century. Portchester Castle is a medieval building constructed inside Roman walls—not an unusual device. There was once an important Roman town at Silchester, relics of which are in various museums.

On the Isle of Wight, Cowes stages the main event of the yachting season—"Cowes Week"—in August. The fine sea views from little Freshwater, on the tip of the island, were once contemplated by Tennyson, who used to read his poetry to Queen Victoria at Osborne, one of her favourite houses, where she died in 1901; it is lovingly maintained. At Carisbrooke Castle, King Charles I was imprisoned before his execution in 1649.

The counties of Berkshire and Buckinghamshire are more closely associated with "the great wen", as Cobbett invariably called the unloved capital, but retain their older character: a town like Wokingham has managed to combined old and new without severe conflict. The Chiltern Hills run from Berkshire across Buckinghamshire into Bedfordshire. Farther south the chalk downs, with a prehistoric path along the top and marvellous rural views, rise higher than anywhere else. "Watership Down", made famous in Richard Adams's picaresque story of rabbits, lies south of Newbury. The Vale of the White Horse is so named for the animal carved in the turf on the slope of the downs. Some 120 m long, this mysterious symbol was made over 2,000 years ago.

The green valley of the Thames, which forms part of the border between Berkshire and Buckinghamshire, offers scenery markedly different from the austere chalk downs or the beech-covered hills of the Chilterns. Maidenhead is mainly residential, and a good centre for boating. At Marlow, with its spacious High Street, there is a suspension bridge over the Thames and a house where the Shelleys lived. Henley (over the county boundary in Oxfordshire) is the scene of an annual regatta, where rowing crews from many countries compete. Reading, the county town of Berkshire, has recently developed into a large industrial and university city; in literature it is best remembered for its prison, thanks to Oscar Wilde's *Ballad of Reading Gaol.* At Mapledurham there is a fine Elizabethan house enhanced by its riverside setting; there is another fine manor house, with a moat, at Appleton.

Newbury is a pleasant old town with strong agricultural and horse-racing interests; the latter are even more evident at Ascot. At Kingston Lisle there is a "Blowing Stone", a punctured sarsen down which, according to legend, King Alfred blew to summon his hosts against the Danes. Bracknell is a new industrial town, complete with by-pass road which must give it more

24

Left, Eton College, the monument to Henry VI. Above, Windsor Castle.

traffic roundabouts to the mile than any place in England. At Sandhurst, the Royal Military Academy trains officers for the British army. Aylesbury, county town of Buckinghamshire, was once famous for its ducklings; it has an unusual church steeple and a well-displayed collection of local antiquities. Eton is famous for its preeminent boys' school, which has trained so many British statesmen. The churchyard at Stoke Poges inspired one of the most famous poems in English, the *Elegy in a Country Churchyard* of Thomas Gray (1716-71).

Among other places of outstanding historical or artistic interest are Ashdown House (a fine 17th-century staircase); Claydon House, Steeple Claydon, containing a museum of Florence Nightingale; Hughenden Manor, near High Wycombe, home of Disraeli; Stowe School, with fine 18th-century buildings and grounds; Cliveden, a mainly 19th-century house formerly owned by Lord Astor and notoriously associated with the policy of "appeasement" in the 1930s; and of course the grand royal castle of Windsor, with its Great Park containing polo ground and woodland gardens. The smallish, mainly brick-built towns of this region nearly all have points of interest; it would be easy to spend a day in—for example—Abingdon without exhausting all the sights.

THE WEST AND SOUTH-WEST

South-western England contains all the elements of the traditional English countryside —charming villages of thatch and stone, rolling pastures, open heath and rocky coasts.

Wiltshire, the link between the south-east and the south-west, is, despite its central location, a lonely-looking county, its towns few and mostly small, its dominant image that of the bleak expanse of Salisbury Plain and the lonely prehistoric stones of Stonehenge, perhaps the most impressive prehistoric monument in Europe. Stonehenge is best seen very early or late, when the shadows are long, the tourists absent, and the fences and car park less obtrusive. Hardly less remarkable is Avebury, north of Salisbury Plain, where an old village is built partly within the massive earth ramparts and stone circles of a Stone Age settlement.

Leaving aside industrial Swindon, with its railway museum and model village, the chief city is Salisbury, built in the 13th century when the town of Old Sarum was vacated because of its poor water supply. The chief glory of Salisbury is the cathedral, unique among English cathedrals because, built in an unusually short time (1220-80), it is stylistically all of a piece, very different from the usual jumble of consecutive developments of Gothic. Its spire, slightly later, is the tallest in England (123 m).

A shrine of a different sort is Wilton House, a 17th-century building partly by Inigo Jones, often regarded as the first English architect. It has

Left, Salisbury Cathedral (13th century), in Wiltshire. Below, the grounds of Longleat House, one of the biggest properties of the Elizabethan era.

Opposite, the prehistoric ruins of Stonehenge (13th century BC); bottom, Wells Cathedral, Somerset. This page, ruins of Glastonbury Abbey, and, below, the famous White Horse of Westbury (180') cut into the chalk supposedly at the point where King Alfred defeated the Danes in 878.

strong associations with the Elizabethan poets, especially Sir Philip Sidney, whose sister was the chatelaine. Another great house, Stourhead, is notable for its gardens, as well as its architecture by Colin Campbell (1722) and furniture by the hand of the great Chippendale himself. Probably more famous than either is Longleat, one of the greatest of Elizabethan houses, with ultra-grand state rooms and park laid out by "Capability" Brown in the 18th century. The Marquess of Bath has greatly increased his visitors by installing a safari park. Fonthill Abbey is a spectacular Gothic fantasy built for the 18th-century millionaire, William Beckford.

The most attractive towns and villages, like Bradford-on-Avon or Corsham, are mostly in the west, on the borders of Gloucestershire and Somerset, where they benefit from the proximity of warm grey or golden building stone. It is the stone which is largely responsible for the charm of the villages of the Cotswolds, a range of low grassy hills in Gloucestershire. Places like Chipping Camden, Bourton-on-the-Water or the ill-named Little Slaughter look as though they might have been made from cardboard for a Hollywood movie, so picturesque and so typically English do they appear, amid the broad Cotswold pastures grazed by sheep and enclosed by dry-stone walls. The Cotswolds skirt the broad Severn Vale, through which England's largest river runs. At certain spring tides the Severn manifests a startling sight called the Severn Bore, when the build-up in the Bristol Channel rolls the waters of the river backward in a kind of tidal wave. Between the Severn and the Wye lies the ancient Forest of Dean, where oak trees grow over a coal field and the local foresters retain feudal rights such as free grazing.

29

Below, the interior of Gloucester Cathedral. Right, Magdalen College, Oxford, and, opposite, Gothic vaulting at Christ Church, Oxford.

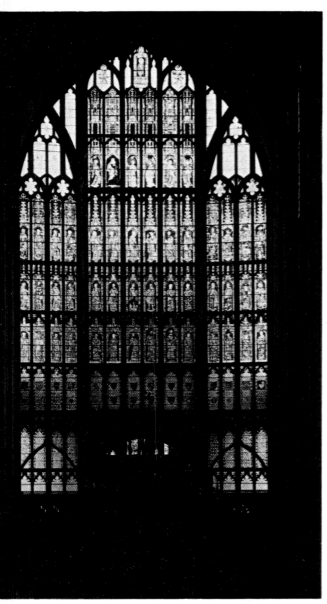

The city of Gloucester was an important place in Roman times. The magnificent, mainly 12th-13th century cathedral was once, like many others, a monastic church. Upstream, where the Avon joins the Severn, the old town of Tewkesbury has a Norman abbey church which rivals Gloucester, as well as old inns and a medieval bridge. Cheltenham is traditionally the preferred resting place of retired Indian Army colonels, though there cannot be many of them left. Bristol is one of several urban areas which have independent status as a county. As the chief port of the west, it was for several centuries the largest town in England after London. From Bristol John Cabot set out to discover North America in 1497. The 18th-century Theatre Royal is one of the oldest in the country, and among other interesting structures is the Clifton Suspension Bridge of I.K. Brunel, designed in 1839. Cirencester was a Roman city, recently excavated; Stroud was once a centre of the wool trade which made this part of England so prosperous—as the many splendid "wool" churches indicate.

Eastward, the Cotswolds extend into Oxfordshire, but the Oxfordshire scenery is generally flatter, though no less varied. The county is dominated by the university city of Oxford. Unlike Cambridge, Oxford is also industrial, with a large motor engineering works which grew from a small bicycle shop. The ambitious schemes of modern planners have been successfully resisted, and Oxford is still a city of "dreaming spires". Apart from certain famous buildings like the Sheldonian Theatre (1669) of Christopher Wren and the Radcliffe Camera (1748) of James Gibbs, the architecture is unostentatious, but the assembly of colleges gives the city one of the finest

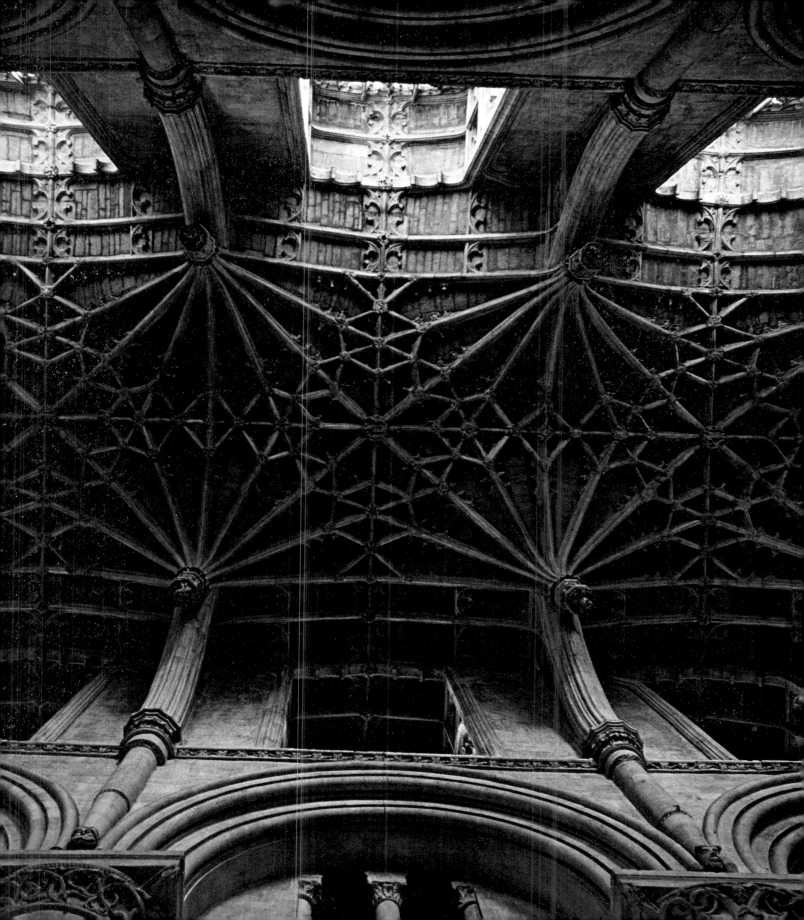

Oxford, the ancient Carfax Tower; the bells of the tower, and, bottom, the august dining hall of Christ Church. Right, Blenheim Palace, so named after the most famous victory of the Duke of Marlborough.

FORTIS EST VERITAS

main streets in Europe, and the many gardens, with venerable trees, provide centres of peaceful calm. From Magdalen Tower choristers sing on May morning; at Christ Church the 7-ton bell of Great Tom, cast in 1680, tolls the curfew. Of Oxford's museums, the best-known is the Ashmolean, with paintings of all the great masters and numerous *objets d'art.* The Bodleian Library contains over three million books, and the Museum of the History of Science has one of the best collections of scientific instruments.

Oxfordshire in general is noted for church spires, which have survived in greater numbers than elsewhere. Of great houses, the largest is Blenheim Palace, by Sir John Vanbrugh (1704), named for the most famous victory of the Duke of Marlborough, whose descendants still live there. During the Civil War in the 17th century the King's headquarters were at Oxford, and there are numerous reminders of that internecine contest—at moated Broughton Castle, near Banbury (where the famous Cross, subject of a nursery rhyme, is a Victorian replacement), at Chalgrove, site of the battle (1643) in which John Hampden was killed, and at the Jacobean manor of Chastleton. A fine 18th-century house, Ditchley Park, by Gibbs, is now a conference centre. Kelmscott was the home of William Morris, and gave its name to his famous press.

The tradition of fine stone buildings continues from Oxfordshire and Gloucester into Somerset, though Taunton, the county town, is mainly brick. The amiable landscape of Somerset owes a good deal to man, and in more fundamental ways than the building of towns. The Somerset Levels were under the sea not so long ago; as marshes they gave refuge to King Alfred in flight from the Danes, but the marshes have long been drained.

Besides the Levels, there are many hills, the most considerable being the Mendips and the Quantocks, which rise above 300 metres in places. In the tortured limestone of the Mendips there are many caves, some unexplored, and more spectacular freaks of nature, like Cheddar Gorge. Cheddar is the home of England's most famous cheese, though not much is made there now. West of the Quantocks, the wide plateau of Exmoor stretches away into Devon.

Somerset has a little light industry in towns such as Yeovil, Frome and the seaside town of Weston-super-Mare, but tourism and farming earn most revenue. The largest place is Bath, which without much doubt is the most elegant city in England. As its name suggests, it was a spa, known to the Romans as *Aquae Sulis.* It achieved its greatest glory in the late 18th century as an immensely fashionable place for London society. Bath remains essentially a Regency town, and it brings easily to mind the numerous scenes from English literature set in the famous Pump Room or among the graceful crescents and colonnades.

A much earlier period of history comes alive at Cadbury Castle, a hill fort that may have been the original Camelot, and Arthurian legend surfaces again at Glastonbury, a very old town graced by the ruins of an ancient abbey. The beautiful cathedral of Wells is remarkable for two features particularly, the array of carved figures on the west front (rare in England) and the remarkable inverted arches of the crossing—a 14th-century device to support the failing tower, but visually dramatic also.

Many people, not only those who live there, regard Dorset as England's loveliest county. Though not large—one can hardly travel in a

Opposite page, Thomas Hardy's cottage in Dorset. Above, left, the Roman baths at Bath and, above, typical village in Dorset (Corfe Castle).

straight line · of 80 km within the county boundaries— Dorset has great variety of scenery coupled with an almost total absence of large towns. The coast is probably Dorset's greatest glory, excellent beaches alternating with rocky coves and dramatic cliffs, but there are also woods and meadows, heaths and farm land, golf courses and stone quarries. Dorset is pre-eminently Thomas Hardy country; there are numerous memorials to England's greatest regional novelist, including his cottage near Dorchester.

There are important Roman remains at Dorchester, but its most impressive feature is the Iron-Age fort, probably the largest in Europe, known as Maiden Castle. Standing on the 20-metre ramparts one can almost hear the tramp of Vespasian's men as they advanced to attack the ancient British fortress. Dorset is rich in such prehistoric and Roman remains.

Blandford Forum and Shaftesbury are attractive old market towns; Sherborne, once the capital of Saxon Wessex, has a fine Norman abbey and ruined castle; Tolpuddle is remembered for its six farm labourers sentenced to transportation for forming a union in 1834; Wareham is a picturesque former port, where King Alfred's ships beat off the Danes. Poole, an adjunct of Bournemouth, is famous for its yachting harbour and has some rich men's houses in an almost Hollywood style. The Isle of Purbeck (like many English "isles", a peninsula) is famous for its stone; Swanage is the main town but the villages of Studland, where Virginia Woolf spent some holidays, and Corfe Castle, with its magnificently sited castle where a Saxon king was murdered, are more attractive. Lulworth is a famous beauty spot, and Lyme Regis a seaside resort of old-fashioned charm. Weymouth, larger, has a fine sea front with Georgian houses, and a road to the high peninsula of Portland, harbouring stone quarries, a naval base and one of Henry VIII's coastal forts. At Cerne Abbas there is a quaint Romano-British curiosity: a giant male figure, with formidable phallus, carved in the chalk down.

The large peninsula in the south-west of England, pointing like a finger of fate across the Atlantic, is divided into the counties of Devon and Cornwall. The heart of Devon is the bleak,

Left: top, old bridge at Wool (Dorset); bottom, the beach and town, Weymouth. Above, view of Dartmoor. Below, the city of Exeter.

high plateau of Dartmoor, much of it infertile though archaeologically rich, but including many farms. Tourism is the chief industry, since Devon is blessed with two coasts. From Beer Head, the view eastward is a broken line of white cliffs; to the west, the cliffs are red sandstone; while the northern coast offers even more dramatic scenery.

Towns and villages are mostly small, often tucked into hollows with narrow, winding roads and high hedges: in the picturesque village of Clovelly the street is so steep that cars are not admitted. The old houses of the gentry, like Cadhay, Kirkham and Wortham Manor, are also small, though numerous, for Devon was once more prosperous, relatively, than it is today. The largest city is Exeter, which provides a review of good English architecture throughout the centuries, including a fine cathedral and a ruined

Left, sumptuous Burghley House, near Stamford, the property of the Marquis of Exeter; top, Dartmouth. Above, St Michael's Mount, Cornwall.

Norman castle. Plymouth, with the adjacent dockyards of Devonport, is the most famous port of the south-west, from which Drake set out to sail around the world or battle the Spanish galleons. Relics of Drake, in the museum of Buckland Abbey, include his drum, which must be beaten to bring him back to defend England in some future emergency. Naval traditions are maintained at the Royal Naval College in Dartmouth.

Crediton and Tiverton are typical old wool towns, as their large churches suggest. Budleigh Salterton is relatively modern, and the scene of croquet tournaments. The bridge over the Taw at Barnstaple dates from the 13th century, and there is an equally fine old bridge over the Torridge at Bideford. Carpets are still made at Axminster and lace at Honiton, while "cream teas" (thick clotted cream with jam and scones) are served almost everywhere. Lundy Island, with its bird sanctuary and seals, attracts hordes of naturalists.

Above, the harbour, St Ives, Cornwall; below, landscape in the Scilly Isles. Right, the village church, Hinton, Wiltshire.

In Celtic Cornwall—the old Cornish language is allied with those of Wales and Brittany—the magnificent coastline continues, reaching the southernmost point of England at the Lizard and western-most at Land's End. The coast apart, the Cornish countryside is a little disappointing —harsh granite moors, though also small fields, sunken lanes, deserted mines (tin was mined in Cornwall centuries before the Romans), and little stone villages that look as though they have grown out of the earth. Comparatively poor and isolated, Cornwall has few great buildings; though its 16th- and 17th-century houses have endured less rebuilding than those of other parts. Cotehele House is a rewarding Tudor mansion, and Antony House, near Torpoint, is a fine representation of the 18th century.

The main towns are Launceston, Falmouth, still a lively port as well as a seaside resort, Penzance, pleasantly Victorian, St Austell, with deposits of china clay, and Truro, with much 18th-century charm. Other centres of attraction are St Michael's Mount, topped by a medieval chapel and cut off at high tide; Helston, scene of the Floral Dance celebrated in a well-known song; Lanhydrock House, with its sycamores and flowers; East Looe, centre for shark fishing;

Mevagissey, a romantic fishing village; Lostwithiel, with superbly situated moated castle; St Ives, where artists in search of light and colour congregate; and Tintagel, with its legends of King Arthur.

The Isles of Scilly—five are inhabited—are a rough boat ride from Penzance. Their sole purpose is to satisfy those in search of sun and sea, but there is a 16th-century castle and the remains of a little Celtic monastery to look at when the sun goes in.

THE MIDLANDS

The Midlands form the heart of England. During the last century or so they have been transformed by industrial development, which has made Birmingham the largest city in England after London. The city contains museums of industry, with reminders of the famous firm of Boulton and Watt at Soho Foundry, and an unparalleled collection of Pre-Raphaelite paintings at the City Museum and Art Gallery. The Protestant cathedral is an 18th-century building in the Italian Baroque style; its Roman Catholic counterpart (1839) is a prime example of the devoted medievalism of Augustus Pugin.

Coventry, to the south-east, is almost at the exact centre of England. Mainly associated with engineering, it has more history than its larger neighbour but was almost totally devastated by bombing in the Second World War. Among the

Left, the nave of Coventry Cathedral; right, the ruins of the old cathedral which was bombed during the second World War. Below, some modern architecture, the Lloyd's Bank Tower, Birmingham.

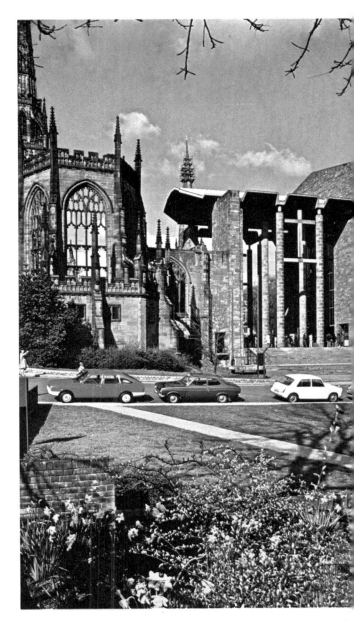

Stratford-upon-Avon. Hight, Shakespeare's birth-place. Below, Anne Hathaway's cottage, the residence of the poet's wife. Opposite page, Holy Trinity Church, where Shakespeare is buried. Bottom, the Shakespeare Memorial Theatre.

casualties was the Gothic cathedral, whose ruins form an attractive adjunct to the new cathedral (1962) of Sir Basil Spence.

Coventry has almost been drawn into the vast urban-industrial mass of the Black Country, centred on Birmingham, which includes towns such as Dudley, Walsall and Wolverhampton (formerly the constituency of Enoch Powell and having a history of racial troubles) and other places of little obvious attraction. But for all the grime of the Black Country, there is plenty of fine and unspoilt scenery nearby. Birmingham is within easy reach of "Shakespeare Country", the centre of which is Stratford-on-Avon, though little remains of Shakespeare's Forest of Arden. The chief attractions in Stratford are the poet's birthplace, the house where he spent his last years (New Place), and the modern theatre of the Royal Shakespeare Company.

Left, the lock gates at Saltford, in the Avon Valley. Above, Kenilworth Castle, Warwickshire.

The valley of the Avon, lined with meadows, mills and bent old willows, is full of charm. At Warwick it is overlooked by a medieval castle, still the home of the Earl of Warwick, whose family monuments can be seen in the impressive Norman church of St Mary. Another castle, even more famous thanks to Sir Walter Scott, lies upstream at Kenilworth, where Elizabeth I was lavishly entertained by her favourite, the Duke of Leicester. Rugby, a sizeable market town east of Coventry, has a famous school immortalized in Thomas Hughes's *Tom Brown's Schooldays.* Compton Wynyates, south-east of Stratford, was built around 1500 and is one of the finest houses of its date in England; its appeal is enhanced by the numerous dramatic events, notably in the Civil War, which have left their mark upon it.

The Avon meanders westward, though the orchards of the Vale of Evesham, past Bredon Hill (300 metres), to join the mightier Severn, the main north-south artery of the west. At Worcester, where the odd salmon is caught, there

Above, Worcester Cathedral, in its pleasant rural setting. Right, Compton Wynyates, one of the most beautiful Tudor mansions in England.

is a power station, but also a magnificent cathedral, mainly 14th-century but much restored, which with the famous cricket ground in the foreground may be seen on many a postcard and calendar advertising the beauties of England. The piquant Worcester sauce is still produced in the city, and so is Worcester porcelain, distinguished since the 18th century.

Near Worcester the Severn is joined by the Teme which, flowing through sandstone from the west, colours the river brownish-red. The Teme runs through mixed farmland, bright with flowers and cherry blossom in the spring, with white-faced Hereford cattle grazing in the meadows. To the south, the Malvern Hills offer views, it is alleged, of fourteen counties on a clear day.

In Herefordshire one approaches the Welsh Marches (borders). Towns are generally small, with many half-timbered houses. Hereford itself has a cathedral of Norman origin (but much altered through the centuries). For unspoilt Norman architecture, the little church at Kilpeck is worth

Stokesay Castle, in Shropshire.

visiting. More formidable constructions are evident in the ruins of Goodrich Castle in the lovely Wye valley, where salmon leap. Ross-on-Wye, standing high above the river, is a centre of tourist traffic, and besides its splendid views and attractive buildings, boasts one of the largest bookshops in England. Besides the ruined castles, like Pembridge, of the Marcher Lords who were charged with keeping the Welsh in order, Offa's Dyke, an earthen rampart built by a Saxon king of the Midland kingdom of Mercia, remains, though somewhat eroded, a symbol of English troubles with their Celtic neighbours.

A somewhat longer section of Offa's Dyke is visible in western Shropshire (Salop), where ranges of hills rise up towards the Welsh border. Much of Shropshire is soft and green, with many lakes, while parts of the west and north are bleak and remote. The Long Mynd is a wild, heathery plateau, completely different from gorgeous Corvedale, a few miles to the east. The Wrekin is the highest point for some miles around, and is associated with many local legends and sayings. To the north there is good dairy country, while pretty Craven Arms is renowned as the place of great sheep sales. Shrewsbury, like Bridgnorth, derives great benefit from its site on the Severn. It has long been an important provincial centre, as its buildings—a sandstone castle, two splendid bridges, many churches and fine 18th-century housing—suggest. At the Lion hotel there are reminders of the old coaching days. Bridgnorth has a funicular railway between the Low Town and the High Town, and a church built by Thomas Telford, better known for bridges, aqueducts and canals. He is commemorated in the name of the "New Town" of Telford.

Ludlow is the most romantic town in this romantic part of the world. In the Middle Ages it was a great military stronghold; today the old castle where the Council of the Marches met is a picturesque ruin. A.E. Housman, author of *A Shropshire Lad,* is buried near the magnificent parish church. Other architectural showplaces in

Left, the beautiful gardens of Hodnet Hall. Below, Chatsworth House, Derbyshire.

Shropshire include Tong, a little town with a remarkable church spire, Shipton Hall, Wenlock Abbey, Pitchford Hall, and the Roman town of Wroxeter. But the county also attracts visitors interested in a more recent period of history, for Coalbrookdale was one of the birthplaces of the Industrial Revolution, where the modern iron industry began. A notable survival of those days is the Iron Bridge, recently restored (in the nick of time), the oldest bridge of its type in the world. With the growing popular interest in industrial archaeology, a large and flourishing museum of industry has been opened nearby.

North of the Black Country, the counties of Derbyshire and Staffordshire include a good deal of dull though important industrial scenery as well as, remarkably close by, countryside of great beauty. Dovedale is in parts wild and lonely; the scenic Peak District is safeguarded by its status as a National Park and by the inaccessibility, except for vigorous climbers, of its most beautiful parts. Farther south are stretches of

Nottingham: the statue of Robin Hood and, below, the entrance to the oldest inn in the country (late 12th-century). Right, Newstead Abbey, seat of the Byron family, Nottinghamshire.

prime dairy and stock-raising country, and the open parkland of Cannock Chase, on the edge of the Black Country. The towns of the Potteries, made famous by the novels of Arnold Bennett, are also associated with the names of Wedgwood, Spode and other Staffordshire potters. The industrial towns of this region generally tend to be identified with a particular product: Buxton, with its elegant Crescent, owes its prosperity to the lime quarries; Burton-on-Trent is a brewing town; Chesterfield, with its curiously malformed church spire, grew up on coal and iron. Derby, home of Rolls-Royce cars, is an engineering centre, and Stafford traditionally a shoe-manufacturing town. Matlock, like Buxton, was once a popular spa.

Some of England's most famous houses are, surprisingly, to be found in this region. Chatsworth, basically late 17th century with 19th-century additions, has superlative interiors and spectacular gardens. Haddon Hall reveals a mixture of styles on Norman foundations. Hardwick Hall, built by a formidable Elizabethan lady adept at marrying rich husbands, is one of the most striking pieces of domestic Tudor. Kedlestone Hall has an Adam facade and Chillington has gardens landscaped by "Capability" Brown. On a smaller scale, Izak Walton's cottage at Shallowford is a place of pilgrimage for fishermen. Similarly, Samuel Johnson's birthplace in Lichfield is now a museum devoted to his memory.

The East Midlands are in general flatter than the West. Nottinghamshire, where much of the land is poor, is coal-mining country, as readers of D.H. Lawrence will know. The novelist, a miner's son, was born in Eastwood ("Bestwood" in *Sons and Lovers*), and his house in Garden Road is open to the public. Coal-mining is, how-

ever, localised. There are fine fiews from the hills west of the River Trent, and some remnants of the old Sherwood Forest, where the legendary outlaw Robin Hood allegedly robbed the rich to help the poor in the late 12th century. A fortunate legacy of the mines is the presence of canals and boating lakes. The Trent itself, once subject to frequent floods that blocked the Great North Road (London to Edinburgh), is a famous coarse-fishing river. The great houses fashioned out of the dispossessed monasteries after the Reformation, known as the Dukeries, are mostly ruined or destroyed; only the Duke of Portland remains in residence, at Welbeck. Thoresby Park is splendid, but mainly 19th-century. Beautiful Newstead Abbey, home of the Byron family, was briefly the residence of the poet. Wollaton Hall, in Nottingham itself, is one of the finest of Elizabethan mansions. Nottingham was once famous for lace; nowadays it has the reputation of an unusually well-planned modern city, but its chief glory is the Norman castle, built on a sandstone outcrop above the Trent. At the now-ruined castle of Newark, King John died, unlamented. Rufford Abbey was the home of an ill-fated heroine, Arabella Stuart.

Farther south, in Leicestershire, is the home of fox-hunting. Such famous hunts as the Quorn and Belvoir still chivvy their traditional quarry over rolling fields, and Melton Mowbray, home of the English pork pie, is still redolent of the world of Surtees's fox-hunting novels. The scenery generally is pastoral and, especially in Rutland (once England's smallest county but now deprived of county status), comparatively unspoilt. Two great motorways carry through-traffic past at a comfortable distance. Oakham is a pleasant, peaceful market town with a 16th-century grammar school, and there is a more famous school at Uppingham, while the technical college at Loughborough, recently absorbed by the University of Leicester, has an extraordinary reputation for producing athletes, as well as engineers. The Duke of Rutland's state rooms at Belvoir Castle are open to public view, as are Belgrave Hall (with a collection of agricultural implements), Stanford Hall (motorcycles) and Stapleford Park (miniature railway). Leicester is a large industrial city with a long and eventful history since Roman times. Bradgate Park, once the home of the ten-day queen, Lady Jane Grey, is a valuable place of recreation for the city. John Wyclif, the pre-Reformation reformer, was rector of Lutterworth in the 14th century. The castle at Ashby-de-la-Zouche figures in Scott's *Ivanhoe*.

Northampton, like Leicester, is a large industrial town with a tradition of shoe manufacturing and an eventful past, but a fire in the late 17th century destroyed most of the old buildings. The round church, one of only four in England, fortunately survived. The countryside in this region to the north and west of London is not particularly distinguished though, like most of England, large parts are green and pleasant. Although farming remains important, there is much industry, and little charms the eye in places like Corby, Wellingborough, Luton, or even Peterborough, despite its fine cathedral. In the rural areas, however, villages like Rockingham or Barnack gain much charm as a result of the ancient and continuing limestone and ironstone quarries from which their walls are built. There are also a remarkably large number of great houses: Althorp, seat of Lord Spencer, which once witnessed a masque by Ben Jonson, Shakespeare's drinking companion; Burghley (Huntingdonshire), built for Elizabeth I's greatest minister; Castle Ashby, a classic Elizabethan house; Luton Hoo, by Robert Adam; the popular Woburn Abbey, an 18th-century mansion with one of the finest of private art collections and an extensive zoo in the grounds; and many more. Bedford is a large market town, home of John Bunyan *(Pilgrim's Progress)* with, unexpectedly, a small Italian section. The church of Earl's Barton has a Saxon tower—the finest example in England. There is a fine church too at Fotheringhay, where Mary Queen of Scots was executed. At Southill, Admiral Byng, court-martialled and executed after the loss of Minorca in 1757 (*pour encourager les autres,* a Frenchman hazarded), is buried.

EASTERN ENGLAND

The eastern counties north and north-east of London are the least hilly region of England, though the land is truly flat only in the Fens. Except for a few comparatively small parts such as the naturalists' paradise of Wicken Fen, these boggy lands where the inhabitants once moved about on stilts have been drained to provide some of the richest farm land in the country. The flat Fenland fields cover much of south Lincolnshire and Cambridgeshire and extend into west Norfolk. Should the English wish to emulate the Dutch they could enlarge their territory further by enclosing the wide inlet of the Wash, which is so shallow that muddy sandbanks are exposed at low tide. In north-east Norfolk there is a region which was once under the sea. A network of rivers and lakes, called Broads, where much of the land lies below sea level, it is a popular holiday region.

Much of eastern England was relatively more prosperous in the late medieval-early modern period, when England's wealth rested on wool, than it is today. Industry passed it by, and it remains largely agricultural. Thus, cities like Lincoln and Norwich, which once rivalled Bristol as the largest city outside London, retain much of their medieval heritage.

Lincoln cathedral, with its three great towers, is possibly the most magnificent Gothic building in England, built on rising ground by the Normans but not completed until the late 13th century. Among the numerous medieval remains are the House of Aaron the Jew, continuously inhabited since the 12th century, and a Norman castle,

Left and below, Lincoln Cathedral, the finest Gothic monument in England.

while the town gate across the main road north is largely Roman. A bronze statue of the poet Tennyson, born at Somersby Rectory, stands near the cathedral. Doddington Hall, an attractive Elizabethan mansion, lies a few miles south-west.

Northern Lincolnshire is divided vertically by the high ground of the Wolds, running south from the Humber estuary. Beyond, a band of reclaimed salt marsh parallels the coast, where there are a number of seaside resorts such as Cleethorpes, adjoining the fishing port of Grimsby, and Skegness, where the air, according to an old poster, is "so bracing" (one could think of less amiable adjectives when the east wind blows). To the south, on the Wash, the tower of Boston church, known as "Boston Stump", mounted a light for sailors in the days when Boston was a major port. It was from here that the founders of a better-known Boston sailed to Massachusetts. Immingham, on Humberside, is another port associated with the Pilgrim Fathers, and now a point of departure for the continent. Gainsborough, north of Lincoln, witnessed the marriage of King Alfred in 868 and various minor contests during the Civil War. It was the model for St Ogg's in George Eliot's *The Mill on the Floss.* Other interesting places include Grantham, with a fine medieval church, 18th-century inn, and grammar school where Isaac Newton was educated; Edenham, with splendid castle and monuments of the Bertie family in the church; the bulb-growing centres of Holbeach and Spalding; and Stamford, with many fine stone buildings. At Epworth, the life of the infant John Wesley (1703-91), founder of Methodism, was nearly cut short when dissident parishioners burned down his father's rectory.

Norwich, like Lincoln, is a fine old medieval city, with a cathedral retaining much more Norman work than usual and an elegant 15th-century spire, the well-preserved keep of a Norman castle (there is another at Castle Rising) housing a large collection of the Norwich School of landscape painters, an astonishing number of churches and many old buildings and streets, like Elm Hill, of great interest.

Though generally flat or gently rolling, Norfolk contains an enormous variety of scenery: lonely, reed-covered coastal flats, where there are bird sanctuaries and North Sea oil installations; heath and woodland around Thetford and the royal country house of Sandringham; the windmill-dotted Broads; and, above all, well-cultivated fields. Great Yarmouth is a large seaside resort with perhaps the largest parish church in England (recently over-enthusiastically restored). Cromer and Sheringham, with fine sandstone cliffs, are quieter. King's Lynn is an architecturally fascinating old port with a church (St Margaret's) even more splendid than Yarmouth's. Some of the small towns and villages are highly picturesque, others more workmanlike; nearly all possess great churches, reflecting the prosperity of the wool trade. A small hamlet like Sall, for example, is blessed with a gem of a 15th-century church capable of holding far more than its population. There are also many older remains in Norfolk, including Roman walls and villas and prehistoric flint mines at Grime's Graves.

Among the most notable houses in this county of great squires, outstanding are Holkam Hall, Palladian but rather grim; Raynham Hall, like Holkham associated with 18th-century agricultural reform; Jacobean Blickling Hall; and Narborough.

Suffolk, Norfolk's southern neighbour (Norfolk = "north folk", Suffolk = "south folk"), lacks its long and varied coast but has an even higher proportion of lovely old villages. The half-timbered town of Lavenham is the archetypal "wool town", though its fame has perhaps made it too well-scrubbed. Eye and Long Melford are also charming. This is Constable country: Flatford Mill, owned by the painter's father and scene of *The Haywain*, is unchanged. Dedham Vale and the Stour valley, in Essex, appear equally familiar to lovers of England's greatest landscape painter, who may also visit the birthplace of Gainsborough in Sudbury, notorious as the original of "Eatanswill" in Dickens's *Pickwick Papers*.

Above, the Swan Hotel, Lavenham, Suffolk. Right, Waltham Abbey (Essex).

There are more reminders of Dickens in the industrial town of Ipswich, the largest port between Thames and Humber, where Mr Pickwick stayed at the White Horse inn. Smaller places of greater interest include Aldeburgh, with its annual music festival founded by Benjamin Britten; Bury St Edmund's, where a Saxon king was martyred by the Danes and one great Norman tower remains of a large abbey; Dunwich, once a thriving port, now mostly submerged by the encroaching sea; Felixtowe, a popular holiday resort; Fressingfield, where the Fox and Goose inn unexpectedly serves food as good as anywhere in England to those who book well ahead; Framlingham, whose castle has figured large in English history; Newmarket, a major horse-racing centre since 1619 (King Charles II narrowly escaped assassination returning from Newmarket races in 1683); Blythburgh, with a staggering wooden roof in the church; Southwold, a charming cliff-top resort; and Ufford, where stocks and whipping post still stand outside the church.

Essex, bounding London on the north-east, has suffered more development since about 1800, and some of the most attractive parts are currently threatened, though the Brent geese have been reprieved from the menace of a new London airport on their favoured marshes. There is a smaller airport near Harlow, like Basildon a "New Town" which has absorbed some of London's overflow. However, much of rural Essex remains, with villages of thatch and timberwork and well tended fields; within 15 km of central London the heaths and glades of Epping Forest offer a welcome breathing space for city-dwellers. At harvest time wide stretches of land are gold with wheat, under the open East Anglian sky (East Anglia, the name of a Saxon, or rather Anglian kingdom, now consists strictly of Norfolk and Suffolk, but the name is often used of a much wider area).

Colchester was an important Roman town; the large Norman castle is built of Roman brick. Saffron Walden is a very old town, with a large Saxon burial ground and mysterious circular excavations known as the Mound, as well as attractive pargetted houses. Nearby is the splendid palace (1603) of Audley End. Chelms-

ford is the county town of Essex, with a fine 18th-century hall and many characteristic timbered houses. Timber-framed houses of the 16th and 17th centuries can be seen at Great Waltham, High Easter and many other places. There are several wooden churches in Essex, notably at Greensted, one of the oldest churches in England, and a round church, one of four survivors built by the Knights Hospitallers, at Little Maplestead. Finchingfield, with windmill and Tudor hall, claims (like many others) to be the most beautiful village in England. But perhaps the most typical old Essex town is little Thaxted, with its famous half-timbered guildhall, superb

stone church (not so typical) and, nearby, a brick Tudor mansion. The house of a great Tudor wool merchant is preserved at Coggeshall.

The Essex coast offers recreation for Londoners, especially at Southend, traditional Cockney resort, and Clacton, with its cricket ground; while Frinton is more reserved, a favourite retirement spot. Walton-on-the-Naze, nearby, is the easternmost point of England, and famous for fossils. Like Brightlingsea and Burnham-on-Crouch (oysters and wildfowl), it is a popular yachting centre.

North of London suburbia stretches almost to the old towns of St Albans and Hertford. There are more "New Towns", like Stevenage and the

Left, one of the oldest churches in England, at Greenstead, Essex. Below, the Peter Pan recreation area for children at Southend-on-Sea, Essex.

earlier Welwyn Garden City and Letchworth, the first zonal "garden city", built about 1903. At St Albans, the Roman town of Verulamium can be seen and Roman artifacts inspected in the museum. The abbey church was founded in the 8th century, rebuilt in Norman times and considerably restored in the 19th century. Francis Bacon's house, rebuilt in classical style in the 18th century, is inhabited by the present Lord Verulam. Of greater interest are Knebworth, originally a Tudor house but extravagantly rebuilt when Bulwer Lytton was a child there in the early 19th century, and Hatfield House, where Elizabeth I spent her childhood before it was rebuilt on the grand scale by Robert Cecil, in whose family it remains; the contents are priceless. The town of Baldock has a fine and—since it ceased to be part of the Great North Road—spacious main street with 18th-century houses. Barnet was the site of a decisive battle in the

Wars of the Roses. At Bishop's Stortford, the birthplace of the empire-builder Cecil Rhodes is now a museum. Berkhamstead's most famous son was the poet William Cowper; it has remains of a Norman castle and, like Haileybury, a famous boys' school. The Palladian golf club of Moor Park stands on the site of a house owned by Cardinal Wolsey in the 16th century.

Farther north, the traveller passes over chalk downs and hills until he reaches the rich black earth of the Fens, extending over 5,000 sq.km. On the edge of the Fens stands the famous university city of Cambridge, also an agricultural and light-industrial centre. The views of the College backs from the far side of the River Cam are among the most famous in England, incorporating Wren's library for Trinity College and the dazzling chapel of King's College, the finest example of the English Perpendicular style—huge

stained-glass windows and exquisite fan vaulting. There are a number of fine Neo-Classical buildings, notably Gibbs's Senate house, and the Fitzwilliam Museum, with its magnificent international collection based on the bequest of Lord Fitzwilliam in 1816. Otherwise, the greatest charm of Cambridge lies in its narrow alleys and peaceful College courtyards.

North of Cambridge, the Isle of Ely was once isolated among surrounding bogs. The Saxon rebel Hereward the Wake held out here and at Thorney in defiance of the Normans. Its position, rising in the distance above the mists, is one of the chief assets of Ely Cathedral. In some ways this is the most satisfying of all English cathedrals. It retains most of the original Norman work, including the marvellously carved Prior's Door, with enhancing Gothic additions in the airy Lady Chapel and the unique octagonal

Cambridge. Above, St John's. Right, the interior of King's College Chapel.

crossing—a device of extraordinary brilliance attributed to Alan de Walsingham in the early 14th century.

Huntingdon and Godmanchester are sedate and Georgian, with nature reserves nearby sheltering rare birds and insects. The Cromwell Museum at Huntingdon was once a school where Oliver Cromwell and Samuel Pepys, the 17th-century diarist, were educated. Hinchingbroke House, home of Cromwell's forbears, is now a school. Pepys's house at Brampton is open to the public, as is 16th-century Sawston Hall, home of the same family since the Middle Ages.

Thatched roofs give the villages of this part of the country special charm. Grantchester, made famous by the poet Rupert Brooke, is one example; it is pleasantly reached by punt from Cambridge. Wisbech, close to orchards and bulb fields, is an undeservedly neglected Fenland town, with fine old warehouses, in need of restoration, along the River Nene, good Georgian houses, and a statue of Thomas Clarkson, the opponent of the slave trade, by Gilbert Scott. At Tydd-St-Giles, near Wisbech, Nicholas Breakspear was curate; in 1154 he became the only Englishman to be elected pope, as Adrian IV.

THE NORTH COUNTRY

Many countries manifest a marked difference between north and south; certainly England does. Northerners are said to be more down-to-earth and more hospitable than southerners, whom they regard as spoiled and effete. The North is poorer than the South, relatively deprived economically and, some northerners think, exploited politically. Historically, power in England has always lain in the south, except for a brief period in early Saxon times when Northumbria was the greatest kingdom in England.

The numerous local foods of the north reflect its comparative poverty: Yorkshire pudding and Lancashire hot-pot are really "peasant" dishes, as are such local phenomena as black pudding, an acquired taste, to say the least.

The North, between the Humber and the Scottish border, can be broadly divided into two sections: the industrial belt, including Liverpool, Manchester, Leeds, Sheffield, with the surrounding moors; and the more rural area farther north, including the Lake District and Northumbria.

Left, landscape in the Lake District, Cumberland; below, majestic Liverpool Cathedral.

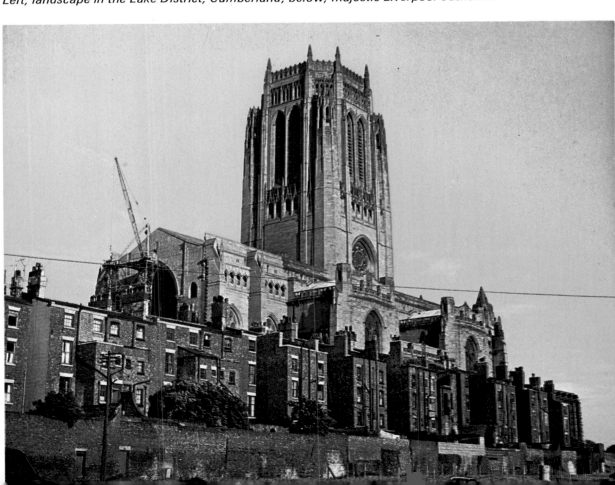

Lancashire, the most densely populated county in England and the birthplace of the Industrial Revolution, is far from being the urban-industrial complex one might expect. It has beautiful hills, extensive moors, bird sanctuaries, attractive villages, rich farm land (especially in the west), and claims part of the Lake District in the north.

From a small fishing village Liverpool rose to be a great mercantile port on the profits of West Indies trade—slaves and sugar—in the 18th century. Merseyside, the docks and the great civic buildings are of outstanding historic interest; extensive bomb damage in the Second World War has been repaired. The Walker Art Gallery is one of the finest public collections outside London, and the two modern cathedrals—Protestant and Roman Catholic—offer a striking contrast in styles. The former, a Gothic structure in red sandstone, was begun in 1904 and completed in 1978; it is said to be the largest Gothic cathedral in the world. The Roman Catholic cathedral, completed 1967, is far smaller but more radical, circular in plan with the altar in the centre, and topped by a tall lantern tower like a scintillating crown.

Manchester, home of the cotton industry, became a major port when the Manchester Ship Canal was built in 1894. The great Manchester merchants never quite aspired to the social pretensions of Liverpool: an old saying distinguishes between "Manchester men" and "Liverpool gentlemen". Like all these great industrial towns, the most impressive architecture is 19th-century Gothic or classical revival. Culture thrives in Manchester, with a fine orchestra, and a theatre in the old Exchange building which has taught London a thing or two. But Liverpool Road Railway Station, oldest in the world, deserves more care and attention.

A feature of many Lancashire towns is an impressive town hall, representing civic pride as churches did in the 15th century. The Manchester town hall, with its high clock tower, is a vast and imposing product of the Gothic revival. Relatively unpretentious towns like Bolton and Rochdale also possess magnificent town halls, seldom mentioned in guide books. Bolton, like Blackburn, has an interesting textiles museum; Rochdale is the home of the Co-operative movement. Lancaster is more obviously "historic", rebuilt, after destruction by the Scots, by John of Gaunt, founder of the House of Lancaster (Henry IV and successors) in the 14th century. Watercolours in Preston's Harris Museum show what an attractive town it once was; the Georgian houses have gone, though a graceful Gothic spire has been acquired.

Of Lancashire coastal resorts, Blackpool, with its famous tower, pier, bands and fairy lights, is one of the best-known in England, the "Brighton of the north". Morecambe also has excellent beaches. Southport is a total contrast, the place, according to an old saying, where Lancashire people hope to die. The main street, with expensive shops, is one of the most gracious in England. Fleetwood is a deep-sea fishing port, depressed since closure of the Iceland cod fisheries.

Lancashire has many fascinating old buildings, though few of the first rank. Rufford Old Hall, now a museum, is a fine half-timbered house of the 15th century. Knowsley Hall, long the home of the earls of Derby, is a hotch-potch of styles since the Middle Ages. The critic John Ruskin's house near Coniston (with a lake once used for water-speed records) is now a memorial to him.

Left, St George Hall, Liverpool; above, Blackpool with the famous Tower (built 1891-94; 520 feet high).

Heaton Hall is a fine 18th-century house by James Wyatt.

Across the Mersey from Liverpool is the peninsula of the Wirral, part of Cheshire. This small county, with much woodland and water, is largely a residential area for the richer citizens of Manchester and Liverpool. It is architecturallly notable for the high proportion of surviving buildings of the characteristically English plaster-and-timber construction. Moreton Old Hall, dating from the 15th century, is a particularly striking, decorative example.

Left, one of the "rows" for which Chester is famous; right, Tudor houses in the historic centre of the town.

Chester is a magnificent old town with a Roman theatre, medieval walls and bridge (over the Dee), much-restored castle and cathedral, and many delightful inns, alleys and corners. Birkenhead is an adjunct of Liverpool, linked by the well-loved Mersey ferryboats. Crewe is a major railway junction, immortalised in a music-hall song. Knutsford, a classy little town, is the "Cranford" of Mrs Gaskell's novel. Port Sunlight was built by Lord Leverhulme for his employees and equipped with an art gallery (good collection of British painting). Stockport is a large manufacturing town once represented in parliament by William Cobden (1804-65), chief opponent of the Corn Laws. Interesting houses worth a visit include Adlington Hall, near Macclesfield; Hawarden, with castle and former home of W.E. Gladstone; Bramall Hall, with Tudor half-timbering; medieval Beeston Castle; and Lyme Hall, where Mary Queen of Scots stayed.

The Isle of Man, in the Irish Sea, has a striking coastline and a mild climate which makes it a popular holiday resort; residents include many seeking to avoid the high taxes of the United Kingdom. It clings to its vestiges of independence, such as its parliament alleged to be older than the parliament of Westminster, and the judicial institution of corporal punishment. More recent traditions include motorcyle racing.

Yorkshire is much the largest of the old English counties (a recent reorganization of local government divided it into three), and the West Riding alone is larger than any other county. The Pennines, a complex chain of hills running north-south, form the backbone of northern England and a natural border between those old rivals, Yorkshire and Lancashire. Heathery moors, picturesque valleys like Wharfedale and Wensley-

The Isle of Man: right, one of the coasts; below, the Elizabethan clock in Castletown.

Rocky landscape in Yorkshire. Below, Little Morton Hall, Cheshire; bottom, York Minster, the largest medieval cathedral in England.

dale (famous for cheese), and pastures with dry-stone walls are characteristic. The North York Moors and the Yorkshire Dales are National Parks—protected countryside. There are major coalfields, good agricultural land in the plain around York, mellow limestone quarries, and chalk uplands which break off in the cliffs of Flamborough Head.

York is an architectural showpiece comparable with Lincoln and Norwich. The magnificent minster (cathedral) is the seat of an archbishop and the largest medieval church in England. The great east window, made in the early 15th century and illustrating the Book of Revelations, is the largest of its date in Europe. There are about twenty other medieval churches in York, a good museum in the castle, some Roman walls, and numerous buildings of historic interest. To the south-west is a complex of industrial cities, associated particularly with textiles (Bradford, Huddersfield, Halifax). Leeds, the largest, has a university with an outstanding library. Sheffield is known the world over for its cutlery, though Sheffield Plate (silver on copper) is a thing of the past. Teeside, between Yorkshire and Durham, is associated mainly with coal and iron, and the birth of the railways. The first public railway ran between Stockton and Darlington. Kingston-upon-Hull ("Hull" for short) is the main port of Humberside, forming the southern boundary of Yorkshire. It was the third largest port in the Middle Ages and, despite redevelopment, retains much of interest, including the museum of the anti-slavery movement in the former home of William Wilberforce (1759-1833).

The coast of Yorkshire is 150 km long. Scarborough is the best-known seaside resort, a spa with a medieval castle, annual cricket

Above, Scarborough, town and seafront. Below, windmill in Northumberland. Right, picturesque view of Durham Cathedral across the Wear.

festival and sheltered bathing beach. Bridlington also combines medieval remains with contemporary seaside fun. Whitby, where the explorer Captain Cook learned his trade, was once a great whaling centre; the Synod of Whitby (664) may be regarded as the true origin of the national Christian Church.

Yorkshire is dotted with abbeys, stately homes and other historic buildings. Fountains Abbey, near York, is the most beautiful of monastic survivals in England. Rievaulx is another fine Cistercian house, as is Jervaulx though, like Bolton and Meaux, it was more thoroughly devastated during the Reformation. The surviving gatehouse of Kirkstall Abbey is now a museum. Beverley and Ripon are graced with beautiful cathedrals, the former, according to local inhabitants, worthy of comparison with York itself. There are important Roman remains at Aldborough, Ilkely and Bowes; medieval castles, in varying states of repair, at Conisborough, Pontefract, Pickering, Middleham, Knaresborough, Skipton and Richmond, which also has an 18th-century theatre. Of great houses, the most impressive is Castle Howard, Vanbrugh's splendid palace begun in 1702. There are fine houses too at Bramham Park (18th century, recently restor-

Left, romantic Bamburgh Castle, Northumberland. Right and below, remains of Hadrian's Wall.

ed), Farnley Hall (paintings by Turner), Harewood House (decor by Robert Adam, murals by Angelica Kauffmann, gardens by "Capability" Brown), Wragby (Chippendale furniture), Burton Agnes (Elizabethan), Gilling Castle and Norton Conyers (the model for Mr Rochester's house in *Jane Eyre*). Harrogate is a famous spa, where the sulphur springs are still in use. Haworth attracts inconveniently large hordes of admirers of the Brontes, who lived at the Rectory. Marston Moor was the scene of the decisive battle (1644) of the Civil War. Wakefield, county town of the West Riding, has some pleasant Georgian houses and a tall (80 m) cathedral spire. Hutton-le-Hole has an ugly name but a pleasant appearance, and a museum of bygone times in Ryedale.

Northward, in Durham and Northumberland, there is industry near the coast, poorish, rolling sheep pastures inland, coal, and forests in the west. The Roman presence is again evident, in archaeological sites, in local museums, and most notably in Hadrian's Wall, the largest single structure of that great race of builders, which formed the northern limit of their empire.

Newcastle, on Tyneside, is a large regional capital, redeveloped with mixed results. Durham is an ancient city with some excellent new housing, dominated by the cathedral, monastery and castle perched on a rocky eminence above the River Wear—one of the most splendid sights in

78

Rustic scene in the Cheviot Hills, Northumberland. Below, Newcastle-on-Tyne.

England, little changed since the 12th century. The cathedral is the finest Norman (Romanesque) building in the country. Among other large towns, Sunderland is industrial, famous for ship-building and glassware. Tynemouth is a resort for Newcastle.

Some of the smaller towns and villages have a rather grim appearance, with slate roofs, harsh red bricks and windy situations (though fine views), but there are also many places of great charm. Hexham is positively romantic, and Alnwick is an attractive stonebuilt town dominated by the—much-restored—castle. Bamburgh and Dunstanburgh castles gain from their seaside situations; Barnard Castle, unrestored, from its location above the Tees. Lindisfarne, "Holy Island", off the coast, was an important monastic centre where a famous illustrated manuscript was created. Corbridge was the site of a large Roman camp and now suffers from quarry development. Berwick-on-Tweed changed hands many times between Scots and English; it has a particularly handsome bridge and a railway station incorporating part of the old castle. Much of Northumberland is good walking country, with excellent beer to be had in the village pubs. There are beautifully sited monastic ruins at Finchale, and no less than four castles of various dates within six or seven kilometres of little Haltwhistle.

Beyond the Pennines, Cumbria fills the north-west corner of England between Morecambe Bay and Solway Firth. The main feature of Cumbria is the large region known as the Lake District; mountains and lakes, luxuriant greenery (this is the wettest part of the country), dramatic colour contrasts, and marvellous views from Scafell Pike and many other peaks. The gorgeous scenery makes the Lake District extremely popular in summer—frankly, it is best avoided in the high holiday season—though the resident population is small, and the life of a Cumbrian sheep-farmer is a hard one. Curiously, the Lakes do not figure largely in the work of major English landscape painters. Cultural associations are mainly literary. Wordsworth was born at Cocker-mouth, where there is a ruined Norman castle, and lived in a cottage at Grasmere, which is now a museum. Keats, Coleridge and Southey all lived near Keswick, on beautiful Derwentwater,

and the house of Beatrix Potter, creator of "Peter Rabbit", at Sawrey, Lancashire, is hardly less popular than Wordsworth's Dove Cottage. Lake-land recreations include boating, fishing, climbing, fox-hunting and sheepdog trials. There is good skiing on the slopes of Helvellyn, a music festival at Kendal, the chief Lakeland town, famous for woolens (hence Shakespeare's "Kendal green"), and a theatre festival at Keswick.

It is the scenery that brings people to Cumbria. Large towns are few. Carlisle, near the Scottish border, is the largest. For centuries a stronghold against the Scots, it is now an expanding indus-trial town, with a much-damaged cathedral and a castle, part of which is still in use. Whitehaven, attractively rebuilt in the 18th century, and Workington are sizeable ports. Inland, there is little sign of industry apart from quarries. The first atomic energy station was built at Calder Hall in 1956.

Above, the Vale of Keswick, Cumberland. Below and right, two characteristic views of the Lake District.

WALES

Wales has been for centuries part of the United Kingdom, but it is not part of England. All Welshmen would like that fact perfectly understood! The Welsh have a different racial heritage, Celtic not Anglo-Saxon, and a different language, as a glance at Welsh place names (unpronounceable to the English) suggests. All Welsh people now speak English, but a sizeable minority have Welsh as their mother tongue (others, of course, speak no Welsh). Finally, the Welsh inhabit a very different kind of country, Wales being largely mountainous whereas most of England is comparatively flat.

The archetypal Welshman is a rugby-playing shepherd or coal miner who sings in a choir. No doubt there are many who perfectly fit that description; needless to say, like any other country, Wales produces its share of doctors, teachers, bus-drivers and shop-owners, some of whom, no doubt, care nothing for rugby football and cannot sing a note. Yet it does seem that the Welsh produce an inordinately large number of singers and poets, who exhibit their art in the annual *eisteddfods* (competitions in music and verse), as well as preachers and politicians, most notably David Lloyd George, the great

Wales: left, typical rustic house. Bottom, Caernarvon Bay, at the mouth of the Conway. Below, cottages at Beddgelert, in Snowdonia.

prime minister of the First World War.

The Romans conquered Wales, though not thoroughly enough to settle there: remains of Roman forts can be found but not Roman villas. After the Roman period, western Wales was occupied by an Irish-speaking people and converted to Christianity by Celtic monks, when the English were still pagans. After suffering attacks by Norsemen and conflicts with English Mercia, Wales was united under Gruffyd ap Llewelyn in the 11th century, something no later Welsh prince managed to do. Wales was never totally subjugated by the kings of England until the conquest by Edward I in the late 13th century, and it was not until the 16th century that the Principality was fully incorporated, for governmental purposes, in the kingdom of England.

The Cambrian Mountains stretch almost the whole length of Wales from north to south. In the northwest, Snowdonia is a National Park, Mount Snowdon itself being the highest peak in England and Wales. Here is truly dramatic

Left, two landscapes in Snowdonia. Below, Conway Castle.

scenery, with many pretty villages among the rugged slopes, and a wild stretch of coast interspersed with good beaches and attractive resorts; Llandudno is one of the most splendid seaside towns in Britain. Telford's famous suspension bridge carries the road across the Menai straits to the Isle of Anglesey. There is another interesting bridge, the iron tubular railway bridge of Robert Stephenson, at Conway.

Farther south the scenery is softer and the population thinly scattered. Another popular National Park is Brecon Beacons—caves, waterfalls and lakes—and there are winter sports in the Black Mountains near the English border. The southwest peninsula of Dyfed is the flattest part of the country, though its stormy capes and headlands form a spectacular coast.

The most populous part of Wales is Glamorgan and Gwent, in the extreme south. Running through the centre of this region is the Rhondda valley, a romantic name for what two hundred years ago was a romantic place. Since then, the natural beauty of this and adjacent valleys has been marred by the imprint of coal and iron,

though the unrelieved squalor of 19th-century industrialism is disappearing and the Rhondda is becoming green again. Cardiff is a major port and the modern capital of Wales, possessing all the civic and cultural advantages one would expect. Nearby, Llandaff Cathedral and the folk museum at St Fagans are of special interest for those concerned with Wales's history. Swansea is the second largest city, for ever associated with the poet Dylan Thomas, who called it, aptly enough, "ugly, lovely".

Wales has many old buildings, of which the most striking are the numerous medieval castles which ring it like a fence—many were built by Edward I to preserve his conquests. Among the finest are, in the north, Beaumaris, Caernarvon, Conway and Harlech, and in the south, Carmarthen, Pembroke and Chepstow. There are others only a little less spectacular. It was at Caernarvon that King Edward declared his baby son Prince of Wales, a title borne by the heir to the English Crown ever since.

Wales is a small country and much of it bears little mark of man. Yet it has many towns and villages of great interest, especially on the coast. St David's is the smallest cathedral city in Britain, dedicated to Wales's patron saint. Milford Haven was an elegant 18th-century town until it became a major port for giant oil tankers. There are lively resorts at Aberavon, Colwyn Bay, Rhyl and Porthcawl, while Aberystwyth is more sober and Victorian and Tenby is still rich in medieval remains. There is a famous narrow-gauge railway at Portmadoc, and the grave of Dylan Thomas at Laugharne.

Of places inland that attract many visitors, Brecon has Iron-Age, Roman and medieval forts. Caerphilly is world-famous for its crumbly cheese.

86

Llandrindod Wells is a former spa. Picturesque Llangollen has a fascinating half-timbered house, Plas Newydd, home of literary eccentrics known as "the Ladies of Llangollen", in the 18th century. Monmouth, the strategic key to South Wales, has a rare medieval fortified bridge as well as other ancient buildings. St Asaph has a well-known cathedral, much rebuilt in the 19th century. Tremadog is interesting as a piece of early 19th-century town planning, and as the birthplace of T.E. Lawrence ("of Arabia"). Wrexham has a remarkably sculptured 15th-century church (and a 19th-century church by Pugin).

Native salmon fishermen on the River Towy still sometimes use the circular boat known as a coracle. The village of Portmeirion is an extraordinary architectural curiosity. The private plaything of the architect Clough Williams Ellis, it is well described by one guidebook as " an ornate and elaborately planned refugee camp for the discarded architectural bric-a-brac of centuries". (But it works!) One final Welsh curiosity: the world's most unpronounceable railway station, Llanfairpwllgwyngyllgogerychwrndrobwllllantysy-liogogogoch. Alas, the line is now closed, and the station sign is in a museum.

Opposite, scene near Brecon, and the Brecon Beacons National Park. Above, the Conway Valley. Left, the coast near Milford Haven. Below, at the Welsh Folk Museum, St Fagan's, near Cardiff.

SCOTLAND

Scotland can be broadly divided in two, the Highlands in the north and the Lowlands in the south, though the Lowlands are in fact more hilly than most of England. They contain attractive countryside, with vigorously rolling hills and much prosperous farm land. Nearly all Scottish industry and a majority of the population are concentrated in the Lowlands.

Scotland's two great cities, though not far apart, offer a striking contrast. Glasgow, on the Clyde, is vast and industrial, the third largest city in Britain and a centre of the—now somewhat depressed—shipbulding and engineering industries. The city centre is essentially Victorian, though there are medieval survivals, including the one wholly authentic medieval cathedral in Scotland. There are other treasures too, like the Art School designed by Charles Rennie Mackintosh, and a fine art gallery. The shipyards lie along Clydeside, and Glasgow's urban sprawl has absorbed numerous neighbouring towns, like Paisley, Hamilton and Blantyre, where there is a memorial museum to the explorer David Livingstone. "New Towns" like Cumbernauld and East Kilbride have been built to absorb Glasgow's surplus population.

Edinburgh, the capital, is one of the most attractive cities in Europe. It deserves its reputation as the "Athens of the North", acquired in the 18th century, Edinburgh's golden age, when the splendid New Town was built in the finest period of Georgian architecture. The city is dominated by the magnificently situated castle,

Left, typical view of the Scottish mountains. Right, Holyrood House, in the noble city of Edinburgh.

Above, panoramic view of Edinburgh and Princess Street.

below which lie pleasant gardens containing a 60-metre monument to Sir Walter Scott, and the main thoroughfare of Princes Street. The "Royal Mile" is a succession of old streets leading from Castle Hill past St Giles Cathedral and many buildings of 17th-century or earlier date (including the alleged house of John Knox) to the palace of Holyrood House, where Mary Queen of Scots saw her Italian secretary murdered. Arthur's Seat, a long-extinct volcano, forms an impressive backdrop, while the spacious cross streets offer fine views of the Firth of Forth between the tall stone buildings. The National Gallery of Scotland has benefited from the skilful acquisitions of its sharp-eyed curators. The National Museum of Antiquities, combined with the National Portrait Gallery, illustrates Scotland's long history; its exhibits include the fearful "Iron Maiden", which

perhaps gave Dr Guillotin the idea for his similar instrument of execution.

Much of Lothian is agricultural, but there are many ancient remains and several fine towns, notably Haddington, which is largely 18th-century. Beside the loch at Linlithgow stands the ruined palace of the Scottish kings. The Firth of Forth has two fine bridges, a modern suspension bridge carrying the motorway and the magnificent iron railway bridge, a masterpiece of 19th-century engineering. At the head of the Firth of Forth, Stirling is strategically situated, its great castle commanding the route north.

The most rewarding area of the Lowlands outside Edinburgh is the district known as the Borders, divided from England by the Cheviot Hills and including some fairly bleak country in the Southern Uplands. The Tweed, a great

Walter Scott's estate, at Abbotsford.

salmon river, runs through it, nourishing small and pleasant towns, like Peebles, famous for their knitwear. In this region too are the remains of magnificent abbeys such as Melrose, Jedburgh and Kelso, and literary landmarks like Scott's home at Abbotsford. Here and there are old houses or castles in the characteristic Scottish style: high stone walls pierced—almost, it appears, at random—by small windows, with occasional turrets or crow-stepped gables.

At Ecclefechan, Thomas Carlyle's birthplace is open to the public. Gretna, on the border, is the place where runaway English couples used to go to evade the English marriage laws. Beyond Dumfries, where Burns wrote some of his best-loved songs, is the district of Galloway, tucked into a corner off the direct route. Red deer roam the hills and the occasional golden eagle hovers

menacingly. There are some fine beaches on the coast of Ayr and magnificent views of the Firth of Clyde from such a place as Culzean Castle, the finest Robert Adam house in Scotland.

The Highlands do not begin immediately north of the Forth. There is rich agricultural land in Fife and Kinross, between Forth and Tay, and fruit growing in the county of Perth. St Andrews, on the coast, is equally famous for its university and its golf; the Royal and Ancient Golf Club is the game's ruling authority.

The Scottish Highlands are comparatively thinly populated, except in the holiday season. Before the coming of North Sea oil, which has made Aberdeen one of the most expensive towns in Britain to live in, the main industry was whisky distilling, still Britain's largest export after motor vehicles. The other main traditional occupation

91

Highland dancing, Braemar, Aberdeenshire.

is sheep-farming; the little black cattle which were the pride of the old Highland clans have gone, although the shaggy Highland breed can still be seen, sometimes kept partly for sentimental reasons.

Some of the finest scenery is easily accessible. Loch Lomond and the Trossachs are within easy reach of Glasgow, and from there it is another short step to the exquisite 18th-century estate town of Inveraray and to Loch Awe, heart of the Campbells' country. Following the single-track road around Loch Awe one witnesses an ever-changing panorama of lake and mountains with, now and then, a grim old ruined castle recalling the violent past, or a deserted croft, relic of the depopulation of the late 18th and 19th centuries.

Apart from the simple enjoyment of the marvellous scenery (weather permitting), there are more specialised attractions for visitors to the Highlands. Grouse-shooting remains an upper-class preserve; it used to be said that no British cabinet minister could be found at work on the first day of the grouse-shooting season. Salmon fishing too, by reason of cost, is rather exclusive. There is first-rate skiing at Aviemore and challenging climbing at Glencoe, scene of a notorious massacre in 1692. The Highland Games at Braemar, including such traditional sports as tossing the caber (a tree-trunk), attract many sightseers in prosperous Deeside, where the hotels are run by polished gentlemen in tartan kilts with very English accents, and the royal family spends a summer holiday at Balmoral Castle. Queen Victoria adored the Highlands and it was partly her enthusiasm that first made them a popular tourist area. Certain old traditions have been somewhat over-elaborated for tourist

purposes. The association of distinctive tartans with particular clans was developed, if not actually invented, long after the clans had ceased to exist as a significant social force, and the sight of the inevitable piper marching up and down at every parking spot eventually breeds a certain cynicism. Nevertheless, the Highlands are large enough to absorb great numbers of tourists without harm, and lovely, lonely places can be found even in the height of the season.

Large tracts of land in the Highlands are innocent of roads, while the many hills and lochs and the indented coastline in the west make travel on the roads that do exist rather slow. In this part of the world, the motor car does not enjoy so large an advantage over the human feet as elsewhere.

Not all the north of Scotland is mountainous. The region south of the Moray Forth is good farm land, largely flat, and devoid of trees, but with a fine coast. There are magnificent sandy beaches up in Sutherland which are deserted even in August, though one would be very fortunate to acquire a Mediterranean tan in that latitude. The climate is definitely unreliable, though it is only in the west that it is very wet, but also surprisingly mild: subtropical plants are grown with great pride in several places.

The far north is divided from the rest of Scotland by a remarkable geological fault, the Great Glen, guarded by Fort William at one end, watched over by Ben Nevis (1,343 metres, highest peak in Britain), and leading, via Loch Ness with its legendary monster, to the city of Inverness where, it is said, English is spoken more accurately than anywhere else in Britain. In the far north, the remotest part of the British Isles, there are frequent reminders of the Norsemen; the Nor-

Left, Loch Lomond; below, the Castle, St Andrews.

Left, landscape in the Shetland Islands. Above, view of Loch Ness. Below, Iron Age dwellings, Shetland Islands. Next page: Tobermory, Isle of Mull, Argyll.

wegians ruled some of the islands until the 13th century, and the old Norse fire festival is still celebrated each January in Lerwick, Shetland. In the Orkneys and Shetlands there are also Stone-Age settlements, notably at Skara Brae, and modern oil installations, as well as farms, fishing villages, and shaggy little Shetland ponies. Tweed is made in the Hebrides, where Gaelic is still the mother-tongue of many of the islanders who, in the absence of trees, still cut peat for fuel. A breed of wild sheep lives on in St Kilda, the westernmost island of Britain. Skye is the most spectacular of the western isles, little changed since the days of Bonnie Prince Charlie, but in bad weather it can be an unfriendly place. Wandering around these remote islands, it is hard to believe one is in the same country as civilized Edinburgh or roaring Glasgow, and breathing in the soft air of the hills and lakes one feels little sympathy for Samuel Johnson's famous sneer that the finest prospect a Scotsman ever sees is the road that leads to England.